D1567129

Dedication

For my husband and boys. Dream big! Anything is possible with love, determination, and hard work.

Clicker The Cat
By Kyla Cullinane

Clicker was a cat

Who loved to play.

If he didn't get his screen time,

It would ruin his day.

Yes, Clicker loved technology and he didn't know when to quit.

Every day, he would log on for HOURS

At night, he tip-toed downstairs to sneak his device.

Only a dead battery could stop his electronic powers.

If you tried to take it away, Clicker would greet you with a frown, "I need to play."

He'd only get up for bathroom breaks and snacks.

Most of the time, he'd be playing all day.

His friend Digi the dog didn't get it.

He'd say, "Come play with us outside.

Ditch your screen, join the fun,

And let's hide."

"We're playing superhero hide and seek.

I'm a ninja warrior. You can make up your own.

My shield protects me,

And I don't want my secret cover to be blown."

But Clicker wanted no part.

"I have to build animal dens,

Explore outer space online,

And cook electronic meals for my favorite hens."

Online is where everyone was.

Clicker just wouldn't quit.

Couldn't Digi see?

It was time for his friend to split.

Digi tried one last time to convince his friend.

"Let's pretend we're breakfast superheroes. I know that's your favorite meal.

I can be French Toast man and you can be an egg ninja warrior.

Do we have a deal?"

Realizing his friend would not give up, Clicker reluctantly agreed.

He'd go outside but play a superhero game?

Not today, he had plans to win in his racing app.

His friends swam with glee while Clicker rose to online fame.

The sun beating down made it hard for him to see.

He fidgeted and squirmed. But nothing seemed to work.

The glare was too strong. And do you know what happened next?

He went berserk.

Clicker catapulted out of his chair

Caterwauling and yowling so loud he barely noticed his

friends' stares.

That cat made a beeline for his screen

Almost missing it completely, in his state of despair.

Luckily for Clicker, his device was still working.

No scratches, or dents, the tablet kept going.

Clicker beamed with pride.

But Digi was convinced that tablet was slowing.

Digi asked if he could take a look, to make sure it was working.

Clicker thought his friend was a thief,

So he said, "No way!

Get your own. This is mine! Good grief!"

Clicker was glued to his device,

He didn't notice he still had sweaty mitts

And his good luck had run out.

The tablet slipped again when the game gave him fits.

It landed on the ground with a crash.

This time Clicker's tablet could not be repaired.

Bye-bye apps, bye-bye screen time.

Clicker just stared.

Now things have changed,

I'm happy to say.

Clicker has a new tablet with rules to obey.

Only thirty minutes each day and only after outside play.

Digi and Clicker take turns choosing games.

Building robots online, racing each other, and pretending to be ghouls.

You see, the tablet is no longer a problem,

Once Clicker learned to follow his parents' rules.

Now the friends play nicely together

Clicker's fussing has ceased

The fun has moved outside.

Well, at least, until a new app is released.

Tips For Tablet Use

"Mom, everyone at school has their own iPhone. Why can't I have one?," he said exasperated. My son was eight years old and not exaggerating. It seemed everyone at his school DID have their own cell phone. Some used it for communication while others used it for entertainment. I didn't have my first phone until I was in graduate school. Clearly, I was out of my element.

Once my son got his cell phone, his requests kept getting more elaborate. Every day, he wanted a new app. He would start randomly Facetiming or watching YouTube or asking Siri questions that would give questionable sites as results. I knew there were parental controls but somehow, he seemed to be getting around them, without even trying. The old trick of keeping the family computer available for everyone to see was not working. Devices and screens were ubiquitous. I knew that I needed to start my research. Based on my research (another book in the works) and first-hand mom knowledge, here are some basic digital tips I have uncovered for keeping screen time under control.

1. Find out what they are watching. What types of devices do they gravitate towards and what are they seeing? Be an observer. Get involved.

2. It's time to talk. Have discussions with your child about the apps they are using. How are they interacting with the apps? Are they educational or

entertaining or both? Do they have friend functions? If yes, make sure they know NOT to friend anyone they don't know in real life. Turn off messaging and search functions if you can.

3. Model good electronic behavior. Use electronics sparingly. Just. Put. The. Phone/Tablet. Down. Or install an app to find out how often you are on your device, be it tablet, phone or another screen.

4. Explain rules of social media. Never reveal your address, full name, school, when you are on vacation, etc. Don't agree to meet anyone you don't know. Don't friend people you don't know in real life. Use the grandma test- if you would not send it to grandma, don't post it.

5. If you ever feel uncomfortable about an interaction, post, message, tell a trusted adult.

About The Author

Kyla Cullinane is a former award-winning news journalist and TV news anchor. She spent ten years traversing the country interviewing everyone from national politicians to local heroes. Graduating university in three years, she won the prestigious Annenberg Fellowship to complete her Master's in Specialized Journalism at USC Annenberg. That's when she bought her first cell phone. It was a flip phone, something her children had to Google.

When she's not penning children's picture book, she's renovating houses as a Realtor ® and investor and baking chocolate chip cookies and buttercream two tiered cakes for her budding You Tube channel.

Made in the USA
Monee, IL
13 November 2019